I0004664

International Baccalaureate

Computer Science HL & SL

Option A: Databases

Part I: Basic Concepts

Important note to the reader:

The specification points for Option A Databases as they appear in the IB Specification document are not laid out in logical order.

It is very important for the student to learn and understand the **basic concepts** of a database before for example understanding the relationship or difference between databases and Information Management Systems.

Similarly, the notion of database transactions, which appears under the 'A1 Basic Concepts' is in fact quite an advanced topic which can only be studied once Information Management Systems have been learnt!

Therefore in Part I we only look at those specification points taken from **across** sections A1 and A2 which are considered as true basic concepts.

The specification points we have used here are NOT in numerical order simply to preserve the logical order of defining concepts.

In several cases two specification points have been dealt with together simply because they belong together.

The remainder of the specification points are dealt with in Part II.

Contents

A1 Basic concepts

A.1.1 OUTLINE THE DIFFERENCES BETWEEN DATA AND INFORMATION

To see the difference between data and information consider the following example:

1	100
2	200
3	150
4	250
5	500
6	750
7	800
8	3500
9	2000
10	1000
11	800
12	600

As they stand these numbers are completely meaningless! They represent some data – as yet we do not know about what.

In order to get any kind of *meaning* out of a collection of data we need to *process* it. This processing is usually done using some kind of application software eg a spreadsheet or a database tool. But it is perfectly possible to process data without using software tools, with pen and paper.

<mark>Information = Processed Data</mark>

If we now plot this data on two axes, it can look like this:

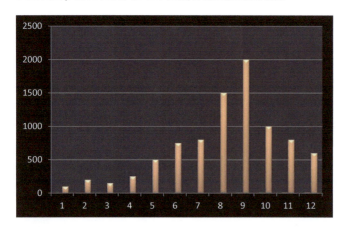

It is now processed data, ie information, but we are still not sure what it all means. Now if we add labels to the x- and y- axes it could look like this:

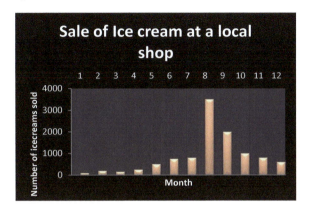

So without any context or processing, **data is meaningless.**

Data → Process → Information → Knowledge

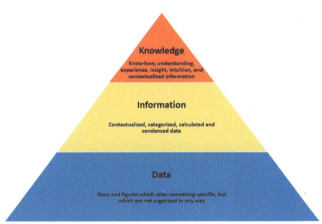

http://www.knowledge-management-tools.net/knowledge-information-data.html

A.1.3 Discuss the need for databases

Access data, search data, share data, transfer data, migrate data

Without databases much of the Western world economies would probably collapse overnight. The huge amount of data processed by companies, organisations, NGOs as well as schools, hospitals, banks, businesses, shops and other agencies can only be done using powerful databases and Information Management Systems.

But just What is a database?

Watch this short clip and answer the questions – you may have to watch it twice.

https://www.youtube.com/watch?v=t8jgX1f8kc4

Use the numbers to stop the clip at the required points to fill in your answers.

0:05 Why don't we ever see databases?

0:15 Where do FB, Tumbler and Twitter put their data?

0:27 Where are the contacts in your mobile phone stored?

0:36 Is a database just a random collection of stuff all squeezed in together?

0:42 Databases have a .... and all the ....we .... in them fits into this ....

0:50 Very simple databases are called ....files.

0:57 They store .... in .... of .... and .... of ....

1:13 What are four things about his friends that Bob stores in his address

book?

1.
2.
3.
4.

1:24 Now write 5 things that Bob wishes to store about Megan:

1.
2.
3.
4.
5.

1:31 The details that Bob writes down are ………….as ………… in his address book database.

1:39 These are the ………… in his database file.

1:46 The information about Megan fills a whole…………… in his database file.

1:54 Each row is called a ……………
Does each row hold data about the same person or about a different person?

2:09 Bob can …………the database file to ……………a particular person.

Source: http://www.123rf.com/photo_19890987_orange-cartoon-characters-connected-with-database-white-background.html

The most important front-end services that a database can provide on a daily basis include:

a. Access data: Data is inserted into tables of a databases. Each table, in a well designed db usually holds data about one object/person/transaction. This data needs to be ***accessible*** by authorised users. By accessible we mean that authorised viewers should be able to view/edit/modify or report on this data easiy.

b. Search data: On a daily basis, we search online for almost anything! Imagine not having the Search facility on Google, or on any of the other apps you use daily….

c. Share data: Just as in the previous point, we share data around the globe on a daily basis. Every clip which is uploaded, every picture, every file which we share uses the share access rights granted to the users of a database eg Facebook for this purpose.

http://www.evolven.com/blog/10-more-cartoons-cloud.html

d. Transfer data: Without the ability to transfer data from one table to another, from one database to another or from one cloud to another much of our transactions on a daily basis would become invalid. How would you pay for your online purchases? How would you book anything online?

"Surely there's an easier way of moving files?"

https://www.cartoonstock.com/directory/e/efficiency.asp

e. Migrate data: Without the ability to migrate an organisation's data from one database or management system to another the organisation would have to re-invent the wheel every time they upgraded systems or decided to move to a new system. Data migration is a very delicate issue, fraught with problems in most real life instances. Typically, the problem comes from the mis-match of data types from the old to the new or in a transfer from one organisation to another (see ETL process in the HL Extension)

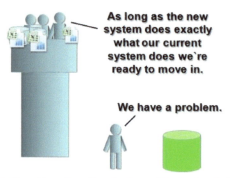

As long as the new system does exactly what our current system does we're ready to move in.

We have a problem.

http://www.datamartist.com/data-migration-part-5-breaking-down-the-information-silos

We now go to Section A2 to continue the basic concepts:

A.2 The relational data model

A.2.9 Define the following database terms: table, record, field, primary key, secondary key, foreign key, candidate key, composite primary key, join.

Definition 1:

table = a 2 dimensional array or grid with rows and columns

First Name	Last Name	Address	City	Age
Mickey	Mouse	123 Fantasy Way	Anaheim	73
Bat	Man	321 Cavern Ave	Gotham	54
Wonder	Woman	987 Truth Way	Paradise	39
Donald	Duck	555 Quack Street	Mallard	65
Bugs	Bunny	567 Carrot Street	Rascal	58
Wiley	Coyote	999 Acme Way	Canyon	61
Cat	Woman	234 Purrfect Street	Hairball	32
Tweety	Bird	543	Itotltaw	28

Definition 2:
Field – an atomic piece of data about a person or object

How many fields can you see in this table?

First Name	Last Name	Address	City	Age
Mickey	Mouse	123 Fantasy Way	Anaheim	73
Bat	Man	321 Cavern Ave	Gotham	54
Wonder	Woman	987 Truth Way	Paradise	39
Donald	Duck	555 Quack Street	Mallard	65
Bugs	Bunny	567 Carrot Street	Rascal	58
Wiley	Coyote	999 Acme Way	Canyon	61
Cat	Woman	234 Purrfect Street	Hairball	32
Tweety	Bird	543	Itotltaw	28

Fields

Definition 3:
Record – a row in a table comprising of one or more fields
How many records can you see in this table?

First Name	Last Name	Address	City	Age
Mickey	Mouse	123 Fantasy Way	Anaheim	73
Bat	Man	321 Cavern Ave	Gotham	54
Wonder	Woman	987 Truth Way	Paradise	39
Donald	Duck	555 Quack Street	Mallard	65
Bugs	Bunny	567 Carrot Street	Rascal	58
Wiley	Coyote	999 Acme Way	Canyon	61
Cat	Woman	234 Purrfect Street	Hairball	32
Tweety	Bird	543	Itotltaw	28

Records

Definition 4:
Primary Key - A field which uniquely identifies the records of a given table.

BookID*	Book Title	Author	Genre
1001	I Robot	Isaac Asimov	Sci Fi
1002	The Cat in the Hat	Dr Seuss	Children

Secondary Key:

Definition 5: A field in a database which can be used for searching – it is called 'indexed'.

For example we can index the FilmTitle field above so that we can run searches looking for given film titles.

Definition 6:
Foreign Key - A primary key which has been *imported* into another table.

Film Directors

TABLE DIRECTORS

DirectorID	Surname	First Name
1001	Spielberg	Steven
1002	Scorsese	Martin

DirectorID is the *primary key* for Table DIRECTORS

TABLE FILMS

FilmID*	DirectorID*	FilmTitle	Rating	Genre
0120	1001	Star Trek	12A	Sci Fi
0145	1002	The Little Mermaid	U	Children

DirectorID is now a *foreign key* in this table

Candidate Key:
To understand the meaning of Candidate Key we also need the definition of a Super Key.

Super Key or **Composite Key:** One or more which collectively identify a record in a table.

Example: In a lending library there may exist more than one copy of a given book. How do we keep track of which copy of the book has been borrowed by whom? We can create a **composite** key made up of the original BookID + CopyID.

BookID*	CopyID*	Book Title	Author	Genre
1001	001	Alice in Wonderland	Lewis Carroll	Fiction
1002	001	The Tempest	William Shakespeare	Fiction

Composite   Key

Join

The idea of join comes from the intersection of sets in naïve set theory and Venn Diagrams.

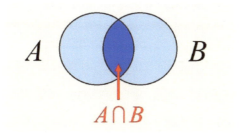

In the theory of databases a **join** refers to linking of two or more tables using primary keys which may/may not be composite in nature.

INNER JOIN

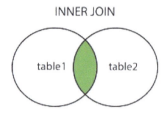

The inner join ensures that the string which denotes a field in one table matches that same key in another table: (this idea is explained in much more detail in the worked example at the end of this booklet)

A.2.10 Identify the different types of relationships within databases: one-to-one, one-to-many, many-to-many.

To understand the idea of relationships in database theory we can consider this example:

One child can only have one biological mother but one biological mother can have many children.

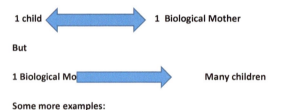

1 child   ⟵⟶   1 Biological Mother

But

1 Biological Mo[ther] ⟶ Many children

Some more examples:

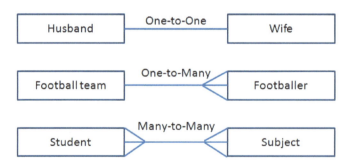

Source: http://fms-itskills.ncl.ac.uk/db/relationships.html

> **In good database design we never allow many to many relationships. These must be broken into two separate one to many relationships.**

Can you break the many to many relationship in the last example above to make it 1 to many?

A.2.11 Outline the issues caused by redundant data. (Orphan data)

Using the example of a child and its biological mother, orphan data would refer to a child whose biological mother cannot be found or traced. Rogue fields of data in a table which have no source or origin are referred to as orphan or redundant data.

A 2.13 Describe the differences between 1st Normal Form (1NF), 2nd Normal Form (2NF) and 3rd Normal Form (3NF).
A.2.14 Describe the characteristics of a normalized database.

These two specification points can be dealt with jointly. We first look at what makes a database be in 1st, 2nd or 3rd Normal Form. By looking at the criteria which are required for each NF we are in fact describing the characteristics of a normalized database.

First Normal Form (1NF)

The rules for 1NF:

- Each data item cannot be broken down any further i.e. it is 'atomic'
- Each row/record is unique and has a primary key
- There are no records with repeating data
- Each field should be unique

WORKED EXAMPLES:

Atomic data

Rule 1: Each data item cannot be broken down any further i.e. it is 'atomic'

State whether the following examples are atomic or non atomic

Data	Atomic or non atomic
Miss Jane Fields	Non atomic
9 Oak Drive, London	Non atomic
Student	Atomic
01926 123456	Atomic
King George VI School Oxford	Non atomic
Supersize pepperoni pizza	Non atomic

Change the following examples of non atomic data into atomic data

Non Atomic	Atomic
Name: Sally Goodwin	First name: Surname:
Address: 9 Oak Crescent, Woodstock, OX2 1AB	Street & house no: Town: Postcode:
King George IV School Oxford	School: Town/City:
Harry Potter 12A	Film: Rating:
Volkswagon Beetle	Car Make: Model:

Rule 2: Each row/record is unique and has a primary key

CustomerID*	Title	First Name	Surname	DOB
001	Mr	James	Smith	14/05/57
002	Miss	Emma	White	21/11/78

Rule 3: There are no records with repeating data

Look at the tables below and answer the questions:

Table 1:

ID*	Title	Surname	Telephone no
001	Miss	Smith	01234 567890
002	Mr	White	01234 890123
003	Mrs	James	01234 798453
004	Dr	Green	01234 578345

Is this table in 1NF?   (Yes)   No

Reason: There is no repeating data

Rule 4: Each field name should be unique

Look at the tables below and answer the questions:

Table 1:

ID*	Title	Surname	Telephone no	Telephone no	Telephone no
001	Mr	Smith	01234 567890	01234 789123	01234 345678
002	Mrs	White	01234 890123	01234 456789	01234 213456

Is this table in 1NF?   Yes   (No)

Reason: Not all of the field names in the record are unique, telephone repeats three times.

How can this be fixed?

By creating Tel1, Tel2 and Tel3 and 3 different fields containing telephone numbers.

Second Normal Form (2NF)

The rules for 2NF:

- The table must be in 1NF
- Non-key attributes must depend on every part of the primary key

Venue*	Artist*	Date	Attendance	Profit	Style
The Barbican	BBC Symphony Orchestra	Feb 2017	3000	$25000	Classical
Wigmore Hall	Mitsuko Uschida	March 2017	1500	$5000	Female soloist

Identify the key attributes in this table:

Venue, Artist,

Identify the non-key attributes in this table:

Attendance, Profit, Style, Date

Does every non-key attribute depend on every key attribute?

No

If your answer above was no, is this table in 1NF/2NF?

Neither

Why?

Answer:

Redesign this database so that it is in 2NF

ARTIST:

ARTISTID*	Artist	Style

CONCERT:

ConcertID*	ArtistID*	Date	Attendance	Profit

Third Normal Form (3NF)
The rules/characteristics for 3NF: • The table must be in 2NF • There are no non-key attributes that depend on another non-key attribute

A 2.1.7 Construct a relational database to 3NF using objects such as tables, queries, forms, reports and macros.

The Driving School Database Model

We use the following record card from a driving school which plans to create a software system to look after its business. The flat file database consists of paper cards which are used to book lessons for each customer.

The stakeholders in this business would normally be identified by the people who run and maintain this business and its related database.

EK Ltd currently use a paper based system. When a customer books a lesson, their record card at the driving school is updated. An example of a record card is shown in table 4.1.

Name:	Nicola Long	Address:	65 Boldmere Drive
			Fradley
Telephone:	0525 555 5555		Lichfield
Mobile:	0725 321 121		Staffordshire
Date of Birth:	14 Dec 1988		WS54 9UZ

| Licence Number: | LONG9 239138 NJ3NR | Date Passed Test: | |

Notes:	Evenings only	Level:	Beginner
			~~Test-Retake~~
			~~Disqualified Retake~~
Passed Theory:	Yes / ~~No~~		~~Advanced~~

| Usual Instructor: | John Woodward | Manual/Automatic: | M |

LESSONS

Date	Time	Length	Instructor	Vehicle	Price	Paid
22-6-07	18:00	1 hr	MW	BX03HMW	£15	✓
29-6-07	18:00	1hr	MW	BX03HMW	£15	✓
6-7-07	18:30	2hrs	MW	BX03HMW	£29	✓
13-7-07	18:00	1hr	PM	BR54URS	£15	✓
20-7-07	18:00	3hrs	MW	BX03HMW	£42	✓
3-8-07	18:30	1hr	MW	BA55WEP	£15	
5-8-07	20:00	1hr	MW	BA55WEP	£15	

Table 4.1 – Driving School Record Card

For each of the fields in this flat file database identify the 'fields'. Be careful – not all of the fields are atomic!

Split the non atomic fields into atomic and determine a data type for each: (some examples are done below, do the rest)

Field	Atomic?	Data Type
Name	Non atomic -Split into Surname First Name	Text/Alphanumeric
Date Passed Test	Atomic	Date/Time
Price	Atomic	Currency or Real
Manual/Automatic	Atomic	User defined
Passed Theory	Atomic	Boolean
Address	Non atomic -Split into: Address 1 Address 2 Post code	Text

For the scenario of the driving school given in the previous section we will now look at normalizing the tables by separating the fields into logical tables. Four tables will be needed in order to put this database in 3rd Normal Form (3NF). They will be as follows:

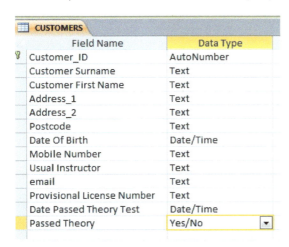

CUSTOMERS	
Field Name	**Data Type**
Customer_ID	AutoNumber
Customer Surname	Text
Customer First Name	Text
Address_1	Text
Address_2	Text
Postcode	Text
Date Of Birth	Date/Time
Mobile Number	Text
Usual Instructor	Text
email	Text
Provisional License Number	Text
Date Passed Theory Test	Date/Time
Passed Theory	Yes/No

CUSTOMERS	INSTRUCTORS
Field Name	**Data Type**
Instructor_ID	AutoNumber
Instructor Surname	Text
Instructor First Name	Text
Address_1	Text
Address_2	Text
Post code	Text
email	Text
Phone	Text
Date of Birth	Date/Time
NI Number	Text
Gender	Text
Date Joined	Date/Time
Employment History	Memo

Field Name	Data Type
Vehicle_ID	AutoNumber
Registration_ID	Text
Make	Text
Models	Text
Year of Manufacture	Text
Transmission	Text
History	Memo
Colour	Text

Field Name	Data Type
Lesson_ID	AutoNumber
Customer_ID	Number
Instructor_ID	Number
Vehicle_ID	Number
Date of Lesson	Date/Time
Time of Lesson	Date/Time
Price of Lesson	Text
Paid	Yes/No
Length (hours)	Text

A 2.6 Outline the nature of the data dictionary.

In order to create our database for the driving school, we first need to create what is called a Data Dictionary. This is a table containing 'meta-data' ie data about data. In this table we simply list the fields as well as their data types and length of each field:

Customer_ID	Primary Key Autonumber	Length of field
Surname	Text	15
First Name	Text	15
Telephone	Text (if set to integer the leading 0 will be dropped)	16
Passed Theory Test	Yes/No (Boolean)	3
Mobile Number	Text	16
Date of birth	dd/mm/yyyy	10
Address1	Text	15
Address2	Text	15
Provisional License Number	Text	16
Postcode	Text	10
Date Passed Theory Test	dd/mm/yyyy	10
Usual instructor	Text	15

Try and choose suitable field lengths for these fields:

Instructor_ID	Primary Key Autonumber or Text	Length of Field
Male/female	Boolean	
Mobile	Text	
Email	Text	
Surname	Text	
First Name	Text	
Address1	Text	
Address2	Text	
Postcode	Text	
Employer history	Memo	
Date joined	dd/mm/yyyy	
NI Number	Text	

FIELD	Data Type	Length of Field
Vehicle_ID	Alphanumeric or Autonumber	
Registration No	Text	
Make	Text	
Model	Text	
Year of Manufacture	Integer	
Transmission	Manual/Automatic (Boolean)	
Colour	Text	
History	Text	

Lesson_ID	Primary Key Autonumber or Alphanumeric	Length of Field
Customer_ID	Foreign Key	
Instructor_ID	Foreign Key	
Vehicle_ID	Foreign Key	
Date of Lesson	dd/mm/yyyy	
Time of lesson	hh:mm	
Length of lesson (hrs)	Integer	
Price	Currency	
Paid	Yes/No (Boolean)	

FORMS

Each table in the database can be used to create a related form. Why should we do this? Because forms make it easier for the user to access the database without having to go into the back-end tables. It is good practice in fact to 'hide' the back-end tables from the users of a database and just allow them to use the forms for data entry.

Forms can be created using a wizard. The Customer Form:

You can make similar forms for the other 3 tables of this database in under 5 minutes using the Wizard tool in MS Access.

QUERIES

A 2.1.9 Describe the difference between a simple and complex query.

Students will be expected to be able to:

- use Boolean operators such as AND, OR, NOT
- create parameter queries •   create derived fields.

A 2.1.20 Outline the different methods that can be used to construct a query.

Specification points A2.1.9 & 2.1.20 will be dealt with together:

Definition 7:

Simple Query – A query which only uses <u>one criterion/parameter</u> to search. For example in the Driving School Database if you were just looking to see how many

- customers have the name 'Smith'
- customers have had 1 hour lessons
- customers have had lessons with Mr Truman
- lessons have been on the 5th of February 2017

and so on.

QUERY BY EXAMPLE

The way to set up a **<u>query by example</u>** is to select the fields required for the query and then to put one criterion down:

CustomerID	Surname	First Name
		='Smith'

Note that if your criterion is text based then it needs to be shown as a string between 'quotes'. If it's a number then it can go in without quotes:

LessonID	LengthOfLesson
	= 1

LessonID	CustomerID	InstructorID
		='Truman'

LessonID	DateOfLesson
	=15/02/2017

Definition 8:
Complex Query – a query which uses more than one criterion and these are joined with an operator such as AND, OR , NOT

Example 1: AND QUERY
Find all customers whose surname is 'Smith' AND whose instructor surname is 'Truman'

CustomerID	InstructorID	Customer Surname	Instructor Surname
		='Smith'	='Truman'

Example 2: AND QUERY

Find all lessons on 15th Feb 2017 AND which have lasted for 1 hour only:

LessonID	DateOfLesson	LengthOfLesson
	=15/02/2017	=1

Example 3: OR Query

Find all lessons which have been taken on 17th Jan 2017 OR 18th Jan 2017:

LessonID	DateOfLesson
	=17/02/2017 =18/02/2017

Example 4: NOT Query

Find all customers whose surname is NOT Smith.

CustomerID	Surname
	NOT 'Smith'

Of course, very large databases use the **Structured Query Language (SQL)** to run queries. SQL is a very user friendly language. To have a look at how queries can be built using SQL rather than QBE have a look at this video:

https://www.khanacademy.org/computing/computer-programming/sql/sql-basics/p/querying-the-table

A.2.16 Construct an entity-relationship diagram (ERD) for a given scenario.

Students will be expected to construct entity-relationship diagrams in 3NF for a relational database.

These tables are **linked** as shown in the diagram below. The 'infinity' symbol means many so the relationships that you can see in the diagram below are all 1 to many.

For example :
1 customer can take many lessons
1 instructor can teach many lessons
1 vehicle can be used for many lessons

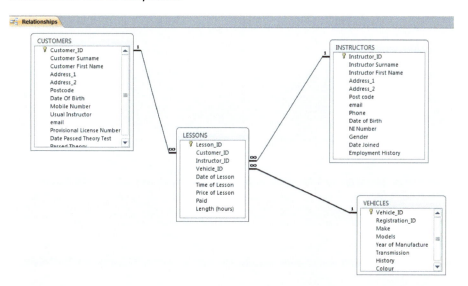

End of Part I.

www.ingramcontent.com/pod-product-compliance
Lightning Source LLC
Chambersburg PA
CBHW041151050326
40689CB00004B/723